D0903196

92
TER

Mother Teresa

A Life of Kindness

Written by Ellen Weiss

Illustrated by Tina Walski

BLASTOFF! READERS

4

BELLWETHER MEDIA • MINNEAPOLIS, MN

Note to Librarians, Teachers, and Parents:

Blastoff! Readers are carefully developed by literacy experts and combine standards-based content with developmentally-appropriate text.

Level 1 provides the most support through repetition of high-frequency words, light text, predictable sentence patterns, and strong visual support.

Level 2 offers early readers a bit more challenge through varied simple sentences, increased text load, and less repetition of high frequency words.

Level 3 advances early-fluent readers toward fluency through increased text and concept load, less reliance on visuals, longer sentences, and more literary language.

Level 4 builds reading stamina by providing more text per page, increased use of punctuation, greater variation in sentence patterns, and increasingly challenging vocabulary.

Level 5 encourages children to move from "learning to read" to "reading to learn" by providing even more text, varied writing styles, and less familiar topics.

Whichever book is right for your reader, Blastoff! Readers are the perfect books to build confidence and encourage a love of reading that will last a lifetime!

This edition first published in 2008 by Bellwether Media.

No part of this publication may be reproduced in whole or in part without written permission of the publisher. For information regarding permission, write to Bellwether Media Inc., Attention: Permissions Department, Post Office Box 1C, Minnetonka, MN 55345-9998.

Library of Congress Cataloging-in-Publication Data
Weiss, Ellen, 1949–
  Mother Teresa : a life of kindness / by Ellen Weiss.
    p. cm. – (Blastoff! readers: people of character)
Summary: "People of Character explores important character traits through the lives of famous historical figures. Mother Teresa highlights how this great individual demonstrated kindness during her life. Intended for grades three through six"–Provided by publisher.
  Includes bibliographical references and index.
  ISBN-13: 978-1-60014-092-1 (hardcover : alk. paper)
  ISBN-10: 1-60014-092-0 (hardcover : alk. paper)
  1. Teresa, Mother, 1910–1997–Juvenile literature. 2. Missionaries of Charity–Biography–Juvenile literature. I. Title.

  BX4406.5.Z8W44 2008
  271'.97–dc22
  [B]   2007014946

Contents

Have you ever known someone
who was very poor or sick?
Did you want to help them?
Many religious groups help
poor and sick people. One such
group is the Catholic Church.
It is the oldest and largest
Christian church in the world.
Many Catholics believe helping
and being kind to others,
especially the poor and sick, is a
way of doing something for God.

Some Catholic women dedicate their entire lives to God. They are called **nuns**. They live together with other nuns. They never marry or have children of their own. Some nuns live quiet lives devoted to prayer. Other nuns work with people, especially the poor or sick.

Mother Teresa was a nun who helped so many people that she became famous around the world. She was born in 1910 in a part of Europe now called **Macedonia**. Her name at birth was Agnes Bojaxhiu. From the time she was young, Agnes learned to be kind and helpful. Her mother took Agnes along to deliver food and money to the poor. She also took Agnes to church each morning.

Agnes admired the priests in her church.
They taught her about helping people
in countries all around the world.
By age 12, Agnes knew she wanted
to devote her life to helping others.

At age 18, she left home to be a nun in **Calcutta**, India. She took the name Sister Teresa and began teaching in a **convent** school. She later became the principal of the school.

Sister Teresa's life in the convent school was comfortable and happy. But she knew many people were suffering outside of the school. Calcutta was one of the poorest cities in the world. Thousands of people lived in houses of mud and cardboard in **slums.** Others simply lived in the street. Poor people drank dirty water and many begged for food. Sister Teresa felt a strong desire to help them.

Sister Teresa decided to leave the comfort of the convent to live and work in the slums. Her life changed with that decision. From then on she wore plain clothes and ate simple food.

She got medical training so she could care for sick people. She started a school to teach poor people. Many people began coming to her school to learn.

In time other nuns joined Sister Teresa in the slums. They began to call her "Mother Teresa" and they formed a group called **Missionaries of Charity**. They gave away their things and **vowed** to be poor. They were kind to everyone.

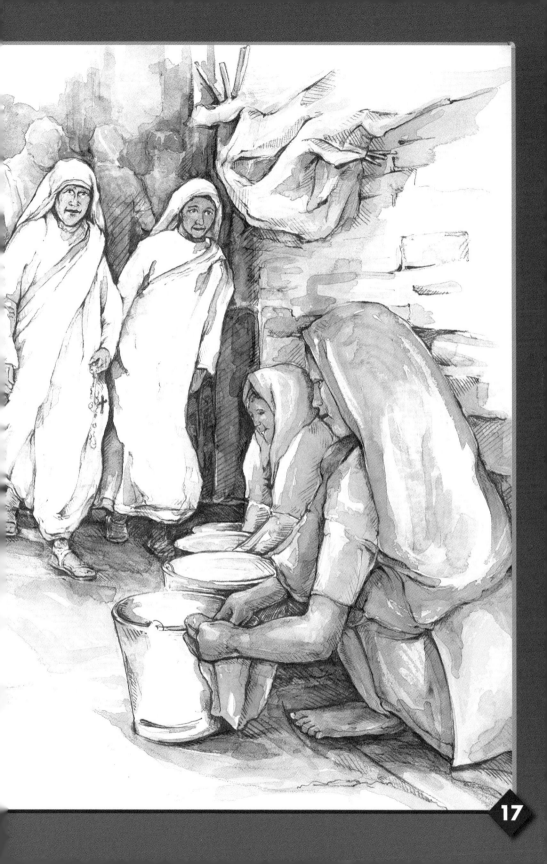

Mother Teresa and the other nuns started clinics, orphanages, and shelters. They also gave food to people on the streets every day.

Sometimes they even gave away their own food and went hungry themselves.

Word spread about Mother Teresa's work. **Volunteers** and **donations** came to help. She won awards and used the award money for her work. In 1979 she won the **Nobel Peace Prize**.

Mother Teresa died in 1997. Her life of kindness and dedication to the poor has **inspired** thousands of people around the world to help others in need.

Glossary

Calcutta—one of the biggest cities in India; Calcutta is now called Kolkata.

convent—a place nuns live and work; some convents also have schools.

donation—something given as a gift to help a person or a group

inspire—to make someone want to do something by showing them a good example

Macedonia—a country in eastern Europe

Missionaries of Charity—the religious group started by Mother Teresa; missionaries are people sent by a church to share their faith and help people in need.

Nobel Peace Prize—a famous prize given every year to the person who has done the most to make the world peaceful

nun—a Catholic woman who devotes her life to serving God as part of a religious community

slum—a very poor and overcrowded area in a city

volunteer—a person who works without pay

vowed—promised

To Learn More

AT THE LIBRARY

Amos, Janine. *Being Kind*. Milwaukee, Wisc.: Gareth Stevens, 2002.

Fitzpatrick, Anne. *Mother Teresa*. Mankato, Minn.: Creative Education, 2006.

Nelson, Robin. *Mother Teresa: A Life of Caring*. Minneapolis, Minn.: Lerner, 2007.

Scheunemann, Pam. *Acting with Kindness*. Edina, Minn.: Abdo, 2004.

Valentine, Emily. *Mother Teresa: With a Discussion of Compassion*. Boston, Mass.: Learning Challenge, 2004.

ON THE WEB

Learning more about Mother Teresa is as easy as 1, 2, 3.

1. Go to www.factsurfer.com

2. Enter "Mother Teresa" into search box.

3. Click the "Surf" button and you will see a list of related web sites.

With factsurfer.com, finding more information is just a click away.

Index